AF430540

Copyright © 2023 Paige A DeLozier
All rights reserved.
ISBN: 9798218115722

feel LOVE give LOVE

written and illustrated by Paige A. DeLozier

This is dedicated to Bryn Adair, my perfect little bean. May you be everything you wish to be, as long as you feel love and give love every single day.

What are my hopes and dreams
for you?

Do I hope you'll be an astronaut
exploring all the stars?

Do I dream you'll be an author
telling stories to the world?

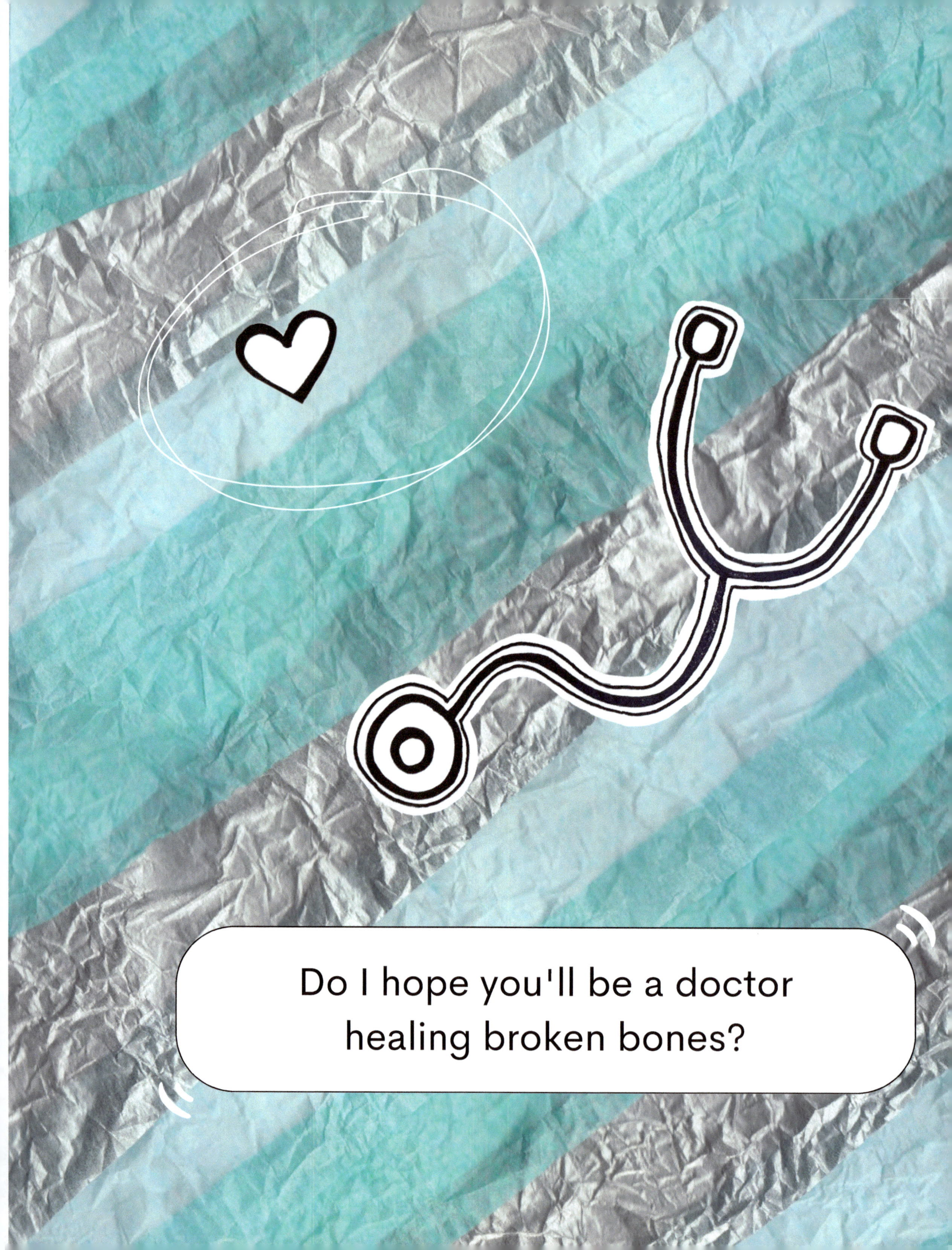

Do I hope you'll be a doctor
healing broken bones?

Do I dream you'll be a teacher inspiring little minds?

Maybe you will do those things.

But what I want for you is much simpler than that.

What are my hopes and dreams
for you?

I hope you feel love and give love.

I hope you feel love...

from the world

from your community

from your family

from your friends

AND FROM YOURSELF!

I hope you give love…

to the world

to your community

to your family

Best
Friends
to your friends

AND TO YOURSELF!

Feel love and give love.

Feel love and give love.

Every single day.

www.ingramcontent.com/pod-product-compliance
Lightning Source LLC
Chambersburg PA
CBHW041948140726
48006CB00002BA/549